Stash books are about freedom. Here, you can do whatever inspires you.

All My Stuff

Scrap paper sections were perfect for highlighting bits from my studio. I adhered everything with regular Gel medium.

The doily, rick-rack & button are from my favorite grandmother; the glass squares from an estate sale.

I collect rusty metal objects. I twisted wire and hammered it flat, then added a rusty washer and old typewriter bits. I painted and stamped wood star shapes. For the tab, I sewed on a big button.

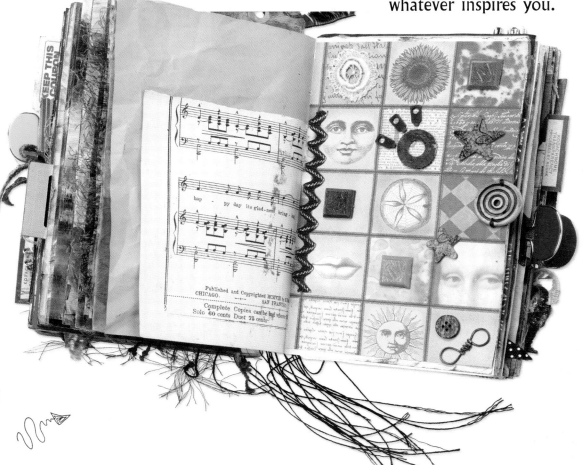

CONTENTS

Getting Started

Take 15 minutes - set a timer if you tend to procrastinate.

Run around the room and gather every piece of paper or small item you can think of that you might enjoy using today. Don't worry about theme right now. Just grab your stuff.

Now, step back and close your eyes. Open them. Grab every small thing that immediately catches your eye and put it in a new pile, preferably on a different table.

Stuff that grabs your attention is screaming its importance. Noticing what gets your attention will help you identify your preferences and will influence the development of your own personal style.

Don't be intimidated by the pile. Let the stuff speak to you. Do you see a theme emerging?

Is there a dominant color? Create small piles of things that go together and start putting them in your Stash book.

1. Collect Inspirational Phrases

Keep your spirits up! Collect inspiring words and meaningful phrases to take care of yourself and instill serenity.

2. Save Coins From Afar

When I travel to countries that use a different form of currency, I always end up with a few coins (usually in the bottom of my purse) to use in my art. Luckily, one of these had a hole in the middle so I set it into the page with an eyelet. I attached the others with regular gel medium.

3. Find a Penny Pick It Up... All Day Long You'll Have Good Luck

Walking from my home to my studio I spied a penny on the ground and immediately recited the "find a penny..." poem. When I got to the studio I stamped and glued a coin envelope into my Stash book. I glued another penny to hold the envelope open. Now I can save all of my "good luck" pennies.

4. Save Contacts

Create a pocket for business cards that you collect - people you want to contact, an art gallery you would like to revisit... or just a pretty card with cool lettering.

5. Add a Binder Ring

Binder rings can be opened to add charms and yarns. You can easily remove yarns if you need to test a color or match a strand.

6. Collect Milagros... 'Little Miracle Charms'

For more good luck I attached a milagro charm to my coin envelope with a small brad.

7. Tie one on! ... or more

Celebrate texture in your Stash book by adding colorful fibers and yarns. I cut these snippets from a fellow artist's collection of great yarns.

8. Personalize Your Clips

Draw a design, write a word, glue a tiny piece of leftover scrap paper. Seal with Diamond Glaze.

10. Favorite Image

Use a favorite image to enhance a photo. Look through a discarded child's book for an image to include with a toddler's photo.

This one has sentimental value - it came from my son's favorite alphabet book.

Make small stacks of everything and start putting them together in your book.

11. Duck Tape!

Use Duck tape to attach an image you want to study for art. I love the characters and color used in this piece. The tape holds it in place but is easily removed if I want to stick it on my art easel for quick reference.

9. Save Images that Spark Ideas

This gorgeous flower brooch gave me an idea for a jewelry piece. I cut it out, whipped out a glue stick and saved it along with my ideas for translation into my own jewelry. Yup, I think I can make it with polymer clay.

12. Clothespins

A trio of metal clothespins adds sparkle and makes it easy to turn the page.

13. Smiley

Adhere a smiley sticker half off the edge of a page. Apply another one on the back.

14. Binder Clips

I love the brightly colored binder clips, and these come with pretty plastic tabs that I can write on.

15. Slide Mount

Sandwich the edge of the page between 2 slide mounts. Putting one on each side of the paper makes it durable.

16. Safety Pins

Insert pins in a page edge.

17. Ribbons

Punch a hole in an edge or top of a page. Apply circle reinforcement. Insert ribbon and tie a knot.

Bookmarks & Tabs

How do I mark thee, let me count the ways! I used 10 different tab techniques to section my book.
Can you spot them all?

SIZE: 6½" x 9½"

18. Cardstock Scraps

Fold a scrap rectangle or circle of cardstock in half. Sandwich a page edge between the halves. Glue in place. If desired, glue a reinforcing scrap of cardstock to each side of the page along the edge.

19. Fuzzy Yarns

Sew fuzzy yarns to the edge of random pages.

20. Button

Sew a large button to the page so the edge sticks out.

21. Tabs with Duck Tape

Cut a rectangle of tape and adhere to the edge of the page. Fold it over to the back to form a tab. Insert safety pins through the tape and attach charms or beads to the pin.

22. Journal Cover

This cover is all about the things inside my book. The matchbook cover is from the 1930's or 40's. The bumble bee and joker images came from an old deck of cards. I used a scrap of old sheet music, and stamp designs on tissue paper.

Tissue Paper Collage

Next time you need to soften a color, adhere a thin layer of tissue paper with matte medium - the tissue will become translucent when it is dry.

Add designs by stamping images onto tissue with Staz-On ink (page 10). Let dry. Adhere tissue with matte medium.

You can apply an additional layer of soft color like Radiant Pearls or Glimmer Mist to add sparkle.

23. Include Meaningful Memorabilia

The coin is from my travels. My husband's airline ticket to Fiji sits beside a palm tree. Because I like wine, I used tiny plastic wine bottles for eyelashes above the eye image. To add texture, I applied the color with my fingers and a palette knife.

Organize Your Stash Book
with Receipts, Tabs and Tags

When you have enough stuff to fill several pages with a particular idea, metaphor, or theme, it's helpful to section off those pages with removable tabs. Try embellishing binder clips. Tie strings to safety pins and paper clips to readily mark your place and decorate your pages.

Layer Your Pages
Papers, Paper Towels, Napkins

Layers add depth and distinction to your art. Next time you view a famous painting, notice the frame. It usually has several layers. The same is true of beautiful architectural cornice work.
Great artists use layering. You can too!

24. Repetition Creates Pattern, Movement & Interest

Repeating a motif, like the red flower, gives unity and flow to the page. Can you find other elements that have been repeated?

25. Handy Bookmarks

So many fibers...so little time!

I smeared acrylic paint and stamped spirals in coordinating colors with foam stamps. I punched 3 holes in the top of the page and applied circle reinforcements then I tied the fibers with knots so the fibers can be used as bookmarks anywhere in the book.

Words, Quotes, Ransom Letters

Cut letters from junk mail, newspapers, or old books to create 'ransom' style words and quotations.

Cords, Yarns, Threads and Fibers

Threads give wonderful texture, color and pattern to your art. Try lacing fibers through punched holes for an interesting effect. I also like to wrap fibers around brads, thread through eyelets and tie to binder clips.

  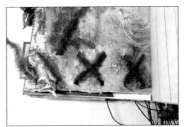

Punch 6 or 8 holes in a page. • Sew yarn through the holes. • Add a second row to make Xs.

SIZE: 2³⁄₄" x 4¹⁄₂"

Using recycled materials as the basis for my art makes me think twice before throwing anything away. Believe it or not, this notebook cover used to be a humble toilet paper roll. The cardboard is a perfect weight.

Screw and Nut Binding

I look for unique ways to use metal. The screw & nut is practical. To add pages, just twist off the nut.

Pages - Make a cover (see below). Cut adding machine tape to fit the covers. Put paper between the covers. Clamp and punch holes for the screw. Insert screw and tighten the nut.

Dragonfly Cover

I glued rice paper over the cardboard. The dragonfly is an imaged stamped on tissue paper. I applied an old airmail stamp and covered the whole page with matte medium.

Inside I store my postage stamp collection. I colored the papers with colors that coordinate with the stamp.

Cover

Flatten a toilet paper roll. Cut it along both sides to make a front and back cover. Paint with gesso. Use your fingers to smear acrylic paints on the surface. Let dry.

Decorate the cover.

Punch a hole for the screw in each cover.

26. Tissue Stamp

Ink a rubber stamp image. Place the stamp (ink side up) on a table. Apply tissue paper over the ink. Use a brayer to rub the inked image onto the tissue paper.

Adhere tissue paper with matte medium.

Back cover

I turn junk mail into awesome papers and you can too - it's free, easy and fun.

Start by crinkling, balling, wadding it up, scuffing, sanding - anything to make it distressed.

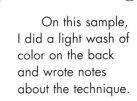

On this sample, I did a light wash of color on the back and wrote notes about the technique.

SIZE: 4 1/2" x 6"

Junk Mail

Artists have a love affair with paper. This is particularly true for the recycle artist, and I am all about recycling.

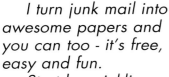

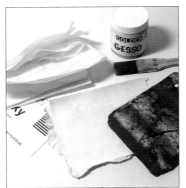

27. Magazine Subscription Post Cards

You know those post cards that fall out of magazines? Don't throw them away! Use them for practicing art techniques - texture, paint, antiquing mediums, gel mediums - anything at all. Coat 1 side of the card with gesso and while still wet, apply strips of tissue paper and apply another coat of gesso on top to act as glue.

This gives a bumpy texturized finish. Experiment with paint, antiquing solution and your favorite coloring techniques. Add a coat of gloss or matte medium.

Punch a hole in the corner and attach a binder ring.

SIZE: 6¹/₂" x 9"

Junk Mail and Envelopes

I had so much fun using window envelopes from junk mail to make the pages of this book.

28. Coloring the Pages

I applied a layer of paint with a brush or with the side of a credit card. Next I used matte medium to adhere images and words.

If the envelope was printed with an interesting texture, I did not paint it, but only glued images to it.

I colored some pages with Portfolio water-soluble oil pastels and used Distress ink in places.

TIP - Alcohol inks adhere to the windows and add translucent color.

TIP - Use an open phone book to support the stack of envelopes when punching holes. Press the fold of the envelopes into the crease of the phone book to keep them stable.

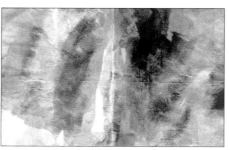
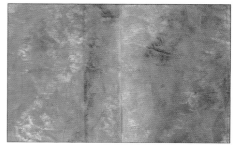

Paper Bag Cover - Use a heavy brown bag for the cover. Cut to size and use matte medium to adhere colored tissue paper to the bag. • Brush randomly with thinned gesso. Smear on acrylic paint, leaving some tissue paper exposed. Let dry. • Apply watered down antiquing medium. Let dry. Doodle with paint pens. Cover with 2 coats of gloss medium.

Tip - When you have envelopes with blue ink inside, adding Gesso intensifies the blue to create a gorgeous color.

29. Doing Nothing

I brushed on a coat of white Gesso. Next, I colored the hair with colored pencils and a wash of acrylic paint with water.

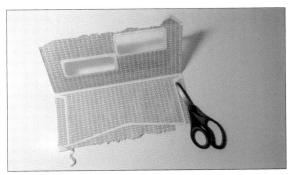

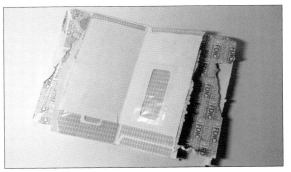

Pages from Window Envelopes - Cut each envelope completely open on both sides and on the top. Because my envelopes had windows, I arranged the pages so there was a window and a blank page on one side, and a blank page and a window on the other side.

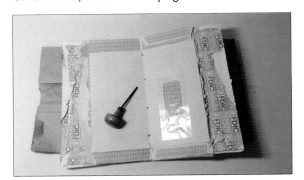

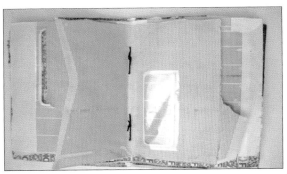

I arranged the pages in a signature of several envelopes. I used an awl to punch 4 holes. Next I used a long needle to sew a binding with waxed linen thread (or heavy-duty buttonhole & carpet thread).

33. Freak Out

When I'm painting, I keep a scrap paper near me for cleaning my brush. Those papers get used in projects like this page. The circles are cut from my "brush cleaning" paper. I used a piece of my own art as the border on the left side.

Every image is from a collection of 1960's-1970's magazines.

30. Mom

I painted thinned fluid acrylic and added drops of alcohol ink. I coated the images with gloss medium.

31. Good Things

Here's a good way to use small strips of paper - glue it down the center of a page.

32. Brut

After applying images, I colored with portfolio crayons and blended with water.

34. Cartoons Collection

These are cartoons from my collection. I added bits of scrap paper to create frames.

35. All It Takes Is A Little Guts

This is the page following the "Mom" page and the window has been treated with alcohol ink.

Managing my Image Collection

When watching TV, I use scissors to clip out magazine images. I like images of eyes and faces so I keep them in resealable bags.

I also organize images in folders in a portable plastic file case so I can take it anywhere. I have several categories- jewelry, crafts, info about artists, travel, nature, abstract art, wine, western, people.

I also have a whole file for napkins and another for greeting cards.

36. Just Images

Airplanes - I cut out images and left the envelope as is. The City Scape shows images of buildings, even through the window. I rubbed soft pastels to color.

37. See-Thru Windows

Here's a great example of 4 different envelope sizes allowing the images to layer.

Resin Pages

This book is a collection of pages of test samples using Ice Resin as the epoxy.

When you experiment with a technique, it's a good idea to keep small samples and take notes about how you did it.

SIZE: 5" x 6"

Dry and flatten used coffee filters with resin. You can also coat lace fabric, bits of gauze, mulberry paper, and vellum for an interesting look.

Cover - Cut chipboard to size and punch holes for the binding with a Zutter tool. Spray the cover with Color Wash inks. Let the colors dry. • Use a sharp craft knife to cut a window in the cover. • Draw on the cover with a Sakura black Micron pen and with a white Jelly Roll pen.

To make the dark swirl, I used a rubber stamp with black Staz-On ink to make a design on tissue paper. You can see how translucent the tissue paper becomes when the resin dries.

Use tissue paper as a base then add the bits leftover when you punch holes in card-stock. Or add blue fuzzy fibers.

Work on waxed paper to apply the resin.

Use rice paper with a swirl. The white stands out against the translucent resin.

On the facing page, I applied resin to a wide piece of lace. The once flimsy lace now feels like plastic.

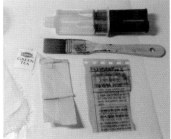

Pages - Place waxed paper on your table. Flatten a piece of lace, a dry used teabag or a scrap of paper. • Following the manufacturer's instructions, mix Ice Resin (from www.object-sandelements.com) in a small disposable cup. • Brush resin on one side of your scraps of paper, lace, etc. and let dry overnight. There is no need to apply resin to the back side.

SIZE: 4" x 5"

38. Grungeboard is Good

A piece of grungeboard had been laying around my studio for a while. I love the feel of it and the flexibility but had never used it before. Ends up it takes acrylic paint beautifully. Apply 2 coats of acrylic paint, stamp and apply a gloss medium. This becomes your book cover.

39. Practically Anything Can Become a Stamp

The feel of grungeboard reminds me of rubber. I wanted to use a tire tread stamp but didn't have one. However, I did happen to have an old tire laying around. I applied black Acrylic paint to the tire and rolled the tire over the red cover.

A Folded Paper Bag for Pocket Pages

Never let a good sack go to waste. Recycle it.

Instead of tossing another sack I decided to see what I could do with this one. It ended up being a great way to tote and show off my collection of ATC cards.

Fold a sack in half (this bag was about 12" by 17"). Fold it in half 2 more times for signature size - about 4" x 6".

Fold it in half one more time for page size - about 4" x 3".

40. Waste Not, Want Not

Make pocket pages from one paper bag. Each page can be used to hold coupons, ATCs or tickets.

41. Velcro Closure

These nifty little black circle Velcro tabs work great for closing the book (grungeboard is flexible and does not stay closed without a little help). Bonus: The Velcro circles are self-adhesive.

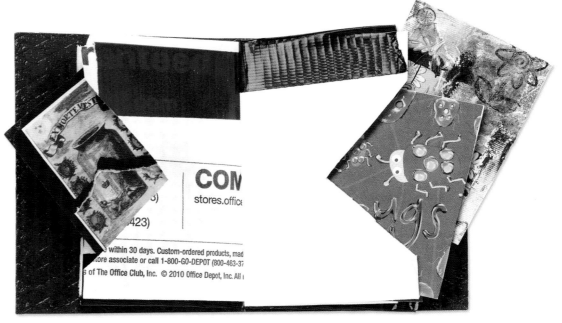

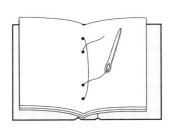

42. Sew It All Up

Use an awl to punch three holes through the grungeboard and through the middle of the stack of folded sack pages. Use a large needle and thin black leather cord, waxed linen or heavy-duty thread to sew the folded signatures to the cover. Tie a secure knot with the ends of thread. Hide the ends of thread between pages.

Cut a large "V" in the center of each long side opposite the center fold. Cut open half of the sides and all folds along the 'V' edge. • Wrap "Duck tape" around the sides to close the openings (I used red on one edge and black on the opposite edge - see photo). • Center the 4" x 6" signatures on the cover. Use an awl to punch 4 holes through the cover and pages. Sew the binding along the fold. • Use waxed linen thread (or heavy-duty button and carpet thread) to sew along the binding. Tie the ends of thread in a knot. Add Velcro dots for the closure.

SIZE: 7" x 7½"

Day by Day

Be inspired every day.

Use a small journal as daily inspiration pages. Display meaningful images and inspiring words.

Turn a page each day - like a desk calender.

44. Carry Images Off the Page

Create interest and move the eye outside of your page by positioning images on the edges.

45. Emboss It

Embossing ink and powder is so fun to use, so many colors to choose from. Emboss a stamp design on your page, or just sprinkle it on.

46. Outline

Outline stenciled shapes and letters with a white Sharpie poster pen or other white pen for extra emphasis. Go around the outside of the letters to make them show up on your page.

43. Graphite Pencil

Use a water soluble graphite pencil to outline images. Smudge the graphite with water.

47. Raised Paint

Embellish images by adding dimensional paint. Red paint adds detail to the lizard.

48. Cut Outs

Save old ads or cards to cut up. Apply to page with a glue stick or matte medium.

49. Photo Corners

Use photo corners on a portion of the pictures. They add interest and create a nostalgic distressed look.

Cut a window opening in a page. Add brads at the top and bottom. Wind wire around the brads.

50. Wired
Wrap wire and brads over an opening in a page.

51. What Does a Photo Tell You?
Love a picture but stumped on how to use it? This picture was used in two ways.
Yellow page - monkeys behind wire bars.
Orange page - monkeys give each other a well-deserved hug.

52. Frame a Photo
I used a plastic cup rim coated with turquoise paint to frame the picture in a bright blue. Continue the colorful turquoise rims on the page for additional color.

53. Rub-Ons
I love this lettering from a sheet of rub-ons.

54. Wrap It Up
Save goofy wrapping paper. You'll be glad you did. Punch circles for this fun page.

SIZE: 3½" x 5"

Words, Quotes,
Ransom Letters
Magazine Clippings

This is a minimal materials experiment. What can I create using markers, paint, stamps, ink, and magazine clippings? Cut letters from junk mail, newspapers, or old books to create 'ransom' style words and quotations.

I used a Strathmore mini journal with 140# watercolor paper, a Tim Holtz book plate and a metal arrow charm to add dimension to the cover.

55. Color Your Pages

Each page was colored with Golden Fluid Acrylics paint. I like to use acrylic glazing liquid to thin the paint and extend the drying time without diluting the color. This allows me to spread the color over the paper to create areas of lightness and darkness.

56. Hush Little Baby!

Use images of dolls to create a fun page.

57. A Study of Faces

How many ways can you depict faces? Searching for specific images enables you to see your travel magazine in a whole new light.

62. After the Party

Scary faces, a carrion bird, and an ominous tree - take your art for a walk on the wild side, escape the ordinary. Your art will become expressive and unique.

58. Tell a Story

Do you know someone who always has beautiful flowers in their home? Use cut out images to tell all about it.

59. Food for Thought

This magazine image reminds me of Marie Antoinette.

60. Patterns with Paint Pens

I happened to see this clipping of a bird in a pile of images on my table. I added the vines and swirly images with Paint Pens. Paint Pens work great on glossy paper.

61. Magazine Border Strips

Mix and match strips of color cut or torn from magazine pages. Tip - I added a funny cardstock hat to the lady.

63. Smile

Here's a stream-of-consciousness page. All the elements are loosely related and designed to make you think.

Zentangle® On-the-Go

Don't leave home without it. You'll never waste time waiting for anything if you have your little book of Zen and a pen. You can tangle anywhere - in the car, on a plane, standing in line for a train... Go for it.

SIZE: 5¹⁄₂" x 5¹⁄₂"

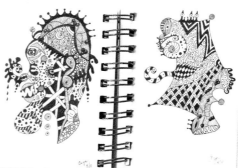

64. Alien

When I was about half done with this tangle it began to look like an alien, so I emphasized the eye, mouth...and I think that's a tongue.

65. Fun Pages

I alternated black and white torn paper to make the pages of my book. I even threw in some red pages to give it pizzazz.

66. Borders

When I glued Zentangle drawings to a page, I added torn strips of black cardstock to create a distressed frame. The binder rings open to add more pages as needed.

I don't actually purchase chipboard. My chipboard comes from the back of a paper tablet or from a legal pad.

The miniature binder ring is a wonderful accessory.

You save a lot of money when you don't throw anything away.

Make Your Own Ring Binder with Mini Hardware

Cut 3 rectangles from chipboard (two 5½" x 5½", one 5½" x 1½"). Adhere decorative paper to each board with a glue stick. Cut each corner on the diagonal. Fold and adhere each side to cover the edges. Lay a piece of 5½" black Duck tape down (with sticky side up). Position the 3 boards on the sticky tape. Secure the ring hardware with brads. • Cover the inside of the board with red cardstock. • Add pages with the edges torn to different lengths.

Having always been a sketcher, Zentangle has given me the right to call my drawings art and even expand on it. Most of my work now includes some tangle inspired patterns. Visit zentangle.com

67. Free Form
Try a curvy, wandering shape instead of a square. Create sections by following the curves.

68. Zen Jester
Can you find a jester hat, eyes, arms and a tail?

69. Looks Like Lace
Zentangle designs grow. Embellish the edges. Note the lace at the bottom.

SIZE: 5³/₄" x 8"

Candy Boxes with an Easy Assembly

These are ideas for things to collect - there's an old birthday card, a Cool Whip container and old game pieces. Even odd shaped pieces can be included.

If you can punch a hole, you can hold it together with rings. Just for fun, I used a scrap of yarn to secure the center. This allows me to tie charms or beads later - when I find them.

Cut a game board to the size you need for the cover. Punch holes. Use the cover as a template guide for punching holes in the pages.

70. Bingo

The bingo card was just something fun. I received a pocket envelope with advertising that I used as the page then I glued images from a Betty Boop calendar.

I kept packaging from the chocolates because I loved the image of the blueberries. I used Candy box tops to make the tabs.

These pages are from my collection of product, cereal and candy boxes.

Optional - Set eyelets to reinforce the holes. Make sure you use eyelets designed for heavy-duty cardstock.

Attach the pages together with individual colored binder rings that are big enough to allow you to open the book so it lays flat.

71. Crunch 'n Munch

This page is a play on words. The image of the boy eating buttered corn is from an old Norman Rockwell calendar. I added images of chilren's faces to the animal cookie box.

SIZE: 5½" x 10"

72. Recycle a Box

The cover for Cinnabun's journal is made from the side of an old cardboard box. I simply cut the shape I wanted. Fold it twice into a form with a cover, a back and a flap.

73. Canvas from the Fabric Aisle

I cut and frayed a small piece of canvas. Next I coated it with gesso then let it dry. I painted it and adhered it with gel medium.

74. Button as a Closure

My cardboard is rather thick so I sewed this button on with wire.

75. Easy Wrap Twine

Punch a hole in the center of the inside flap, knot some twine to wrap around the sewn button to finish the book closure.

Pet Portrait Journal

Last year I lost my beloved bulldog, Cinnabun. Of course I had to journal about it, so I decided that I would journal about her life from Cinnabun's viewpoint. It was very cathartic and gave me lots of good memories. That is one of the best things about journaling - the memories are right there in front of you.

Cover and Pages - I started out using a pallette knife to scrape blue paint onto watercolor paper. • I mixed Fluid Acrylic paints with Glazing liquid and applied color with a brush. • After blending the Fluid Acrylics, I glued images from magazine pages and scrap paper. • To finish, I added Gesso and blue paint.

76. Draw Your Own Images

You can't always get what you want from a stamp or other image. It's fun to have your own drawings in your journal.

Tip: It may take practice. When you get the perfect image on a practice page, cut it out and adhere that to the page. If your drawing is like mine you may not be able to replicate it.

77. Baby Wipes

I use Baby Wipes to move the color around as I apply Fluid acrylic paints freely wherever I want. I use Wipes to blend colors together where one color meets another.

78. Trifold Inside Pages

The inside of the journal is 9½" x 14" 140# watercolor paper folded twice to make an envelope book.

79. Save Funny Pictures

Cut up calenders, magazines and cards for images and shapes.

80. Paint Pens

Paint pens are permanent and many are super glossy. I love to add spirals and other flourishes on my pages.

Steampunk Journal

Steampunk is a new genre of artistic expression which melds with my esthetic of exalting the mundane. Steampunk art is recycled art with a twist. Try to imagine how a Victorian person living in the age of steam power and trains would put something together.

Apply a dash of inspiration from Jules Verne and H.G. Wells. Add whimsy and a heaping cup of creativity. The result is inventive, innovative and fun.

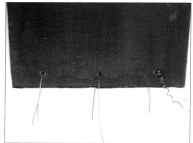
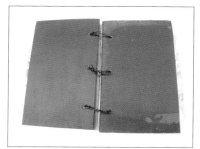

How I Did It - Use the cover from an old book. The pages are my old artwork that was lying around the studio, along with a few pages from the book. I tore the pages to fit. I clamped the book and pages and used a drill press to drill the holes. • To keep everything in place, I inserted a small wire in each hole and bent it. • I then inserted a longer wire and carefully formed a ring, wrapping to secure. Keep the wire wrap to a minimum because the wrap prevents the book from opening. Cover wire with fibers. Attach charms to the fibers.

Decorate the Cover - Apply a few layers of Fluid acrylic paints. Adhere tissue printed with watch faces. • Apply more colors of paint. • Paint chipboard gears and drill holes in the cover. Attach to cover with brads or gel medium. Stamp "steampunk" in StazOn ink. Spray with an acrylic sealer.

81. Spinners

Use chipboard arrow and gear shapes and attach them with brads for movement.

82. Safety Pins

Punch a small hole in the page, insert pin. TIP - Attach a paper note or ribbon to the safety pin.

83. Bookmarks

Tie a cord or ribbon to the binding wire with a knot.

Recipe for Rust

Rusty metal adds grit and a sense of nostalgia to a project.

Dump 1 pound of rock salt into a glass container. Add metal pieces. Cover with vinegar. Wait 2 days. Remove metal and air dry on an old tarp.

SIZE: 5½" x 8½"

Here's a great way to mend the edges of pages.

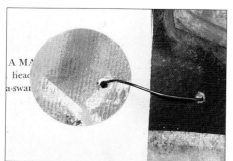

Leather Fringe Tabs -
Staple or tape leftover bits of leather to the edge of the page, extending beyond the edge. Cut the extending edge into fringe.

84. Circle Reinforcements
The paper from this book was so old it was crumbling. Because the book was already put together, I made a split circle reinforcement. First, I punched a 1" paper circle. I then punched a hole a little off center and cut a slit from the edge of the circle to the hole. I positioned the circle, aligning the holes and glued it in place.

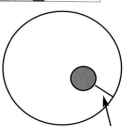

Cut a slit

85. Cheesecloth Secret Page

I began with a piece of my trash art, covered it with scrap paper and rubbed it with paint. I used Pearl Ex powders to rub into the page to add shimmer. Duck tape a feather to the page. Adhere a wildflower with gel medium. I used a white gel pen to make a note. To make this a secret, I soaked cheesecloth in coffee and walnut ink. After it dried, I atttached to the top and bottom with brads.

Steampunk Journal Pages

86. Circle Frames

Punch circles in pieces of scrap paper. Place the frames over photos then glue them on the page.

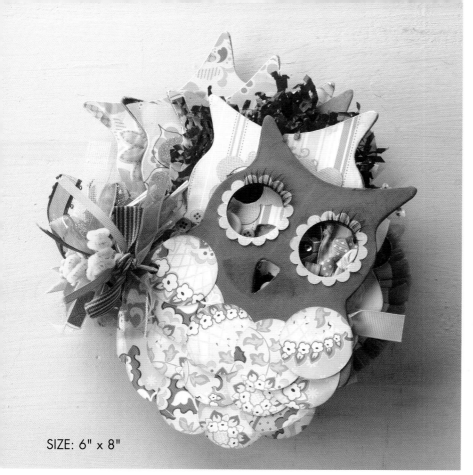

SIZE: 6" x 8"

Owl Book

by Jennifer Priest

Scrapbookers have been making their own version of Stash books for a long time. Thick, dimensional albums are held together with binder rings and decorated to the nines! Check out the ribbons on the binder ring - there are over a dozen delicious textures.

The cute cover gives a hint of the creativity and style to be found within. This is a must-open album.

MATERIALS:

Best Creation 'Owl book' • Decorative papers • Embellishments • Autumn Leaves (decorative paper, felt diecut) • Flowers • Chipboard letters • Buttons • Charms • Ribbons, fibers, yarns • Chenille stems • Rubber stamps • Ink pad • Doll needle, 3-4" long • 6-ply floss • 2 yards each of light pink and dark pink crepe paper • Adhesive

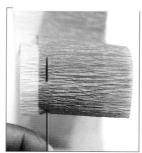

Fold a 2-yard piece of crepe paper in half to make a 1-yard length (2 layers thick). • Lay the dark pink crepe paper on top of the light pink with light pink extending ¼" beyond the edge. • Starting from the fold and using a doll needle, sew a Running stitch along the edge of the dark pink. • Stitch as close to the edge as possible – If you have more than ⅜" of paper between the stitch and the edge of the crepe paper, it will be difficult to create a perfect rosette. Gather the layers while stitching.• Turn the gathered layers over to check that the layers look as desired while stitching.

INSTRUCTIONS:

Front Cover - Punch 1¾" circles and layer them as feathers. Apply a 2" scallop sticker (with a hole in the center) around each eyehole. Adhere eyelashes.

Binder Ring - Ribbons, fibers and curled chenille stems add color and texture.

'K' in Rosette - Instructions for making the crepe paper rosette are below. Lift the ribbon tab (on one side of the rosette) to see 3 layers of photos and fun journaling.

Glitter - Sparkling sequins, gems and glitter accents really punch up these pages.

Photos on the Last Pages - Wrap up the book with a page of journaling and some group photos. Accent with cut out papers, rubber stamps, buttons and gems.

Jennifer Priest - Jennifer is a popular and talented designer who loves to create fabulous scrapbook pages and mini albums.

Her blog is hydrangeahippo.blogspot.com. She can be contacted at hydrangeahippo@yahoo.com.

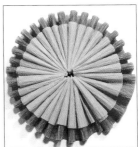

Continue stitching along the entire length of crepe paper. If one length is shorter than the other, trim both to the same length. • When finished stitching, pull the ends of the thread together and encourage the layers to form a rosette by coaxing them into the circle shape. • Tie a knot and trim threads. • The finished rosette should look like this: The longer the stitches, the taller the folds in the rosette. • Add the rosette to your project as desired. Place a chipboard 'k' in the center

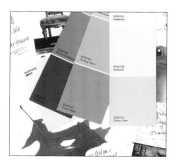

87. Plan a Room

Grab some paint samples leftover from painting a room. Use an eyelet or brad to hold them on a page.

Bonus: Fan the color swatches out for comparison and keep them all in one place.

88. Color Choices

Look for colors you like in leaves, paintings... or geckos.

89. Doodles

Finished with painting your room? Doodle on your paint samples.

Collect color swatches. Stack or fan them out. Attach paper swatches with an eyelet or with a brad.

Garden Delights

My backyard is a wonderful forest - full of flowers, trees, critters, love... and inspiration.

90. Plan a Garden

Save a couple pages in your book for garden plans and places to order seeds. Use empty seed packets as a pocket to store your plans.

91. Add Fabric

Old swatches of fabric from Grandma's drawer are glued on, sewn on and pinned on with a safety pin.

92. Button, Button

Sew old buttons on a page. These were from my grandmother's sewing drawer. Some of them hold scraps of fabric on the page.

93. Write About It

Make notes on the page relating why an image or item is a special memory for you.

94. Photocopy Bulky Items

Have a special item that is too bulky for a page? Make a photocopy then glue it onto your page.

95. Game Night with the Family

Our family enjoys a good game. Monopoly is a favorite. This is from an old game where pieces were missing.

I made a page celebrating the good times with family.

Also I actually decoupaged some of the monopoly money to my game room floor.

Color Your World

What's your favorite color? Do you see it in your art? Note color combinations that appeal to you and record them in your book.

Save Your Papers

Use your stash of orphan scrapbook and craft papers.

96. Page Tab

Use one of the cards from the game as a page tab. Monopoly money or a deed card would work too.

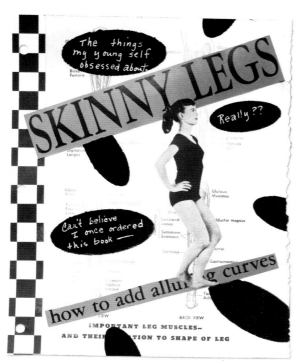

Blast from My Past

I had saved this silly book since I was thirteen. Hard to believe that I once worried about my legs being too skinny...

101. Paint Word Bubbles

Dab paint through an oval or circular stencil to create word bubbles. Use a white Gel pen to write in the bubbles.

102. Reinforce Thin Pages

Here's another use for leftover papers. Reinforce the edge of the paper where the holes are punched (checkerboard paper area).

97. Colored Spray Mists

Spray mists are perfect for a quick change on your page. Set a stencil on top of the page and spray, then rearrange the stencil and spray with a second color. There are many colored mists available.

I love the Adirondack reinkers, they are heavily pigmented and come in so many cool colors. Tip - Just add a few squirts to the water in a spray bottle. (Keep spray bottles from other products you use, they come in really handy for all types of art).

98. Keep an Ongoing List

Cut small sizes of paper to use as a list for the art supplies you may need. Attach these notes to your page with a brad. Rip out the lists as you head to the art store.

99. Gesso Over a Stencil

Dress up your plain papers, lay a stencil on the page and sponge on some Gesso through the openings.

100. Label It

Use scraps from the pocket paper to label the page.

103. Wish List

Clip on additional supplies for your wish list.

104. Coupon Organizer

Always have your coupons handy. Make a pocket for storing coupons on the same page as your list.

Cupcake Flowers

Use cupcake papers to make flower shapes. Add button centers.

105. Fit the Theme

Cut cupcake papers into flower shapes. Layer flowers inside of cupcake papers with buttons.

106. Stickers

Do you have favorite stickers that you have had forever? This is the place to use them.

107. Local Business

Have you ever seen an ad and thought, 'Wow, I want to try that'? Then you forget.

Clip it out, make a note of the name and why you want to visit. I remember that this local winery has a tasting room.

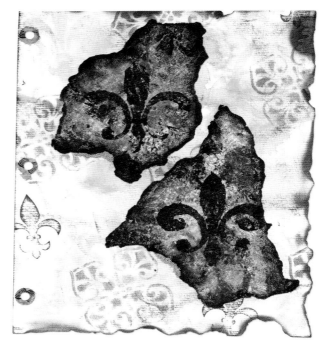

Reinforcements

I inked and stamped these paper reinforcement circles so they are ready to pull off the backing sheet when I need to reinforce a hole. Play with colors and have fun.

Use paper reinforcements (from an office supply). Leave them on the strip. Color with acrylic paint and stamp images with permanent ink. Apply a Clear Sealer - either spray or brush on.

108. Fleur de Lis Tee and Page

I did a project called 'Fleur de Tee' in which I gessoed on my old T-shirt then applied splotches of acrylic paint. I used acrylics to stamp the fleur de lis image then burned the fabric edges (be careful).

The page background is watercolor paper that I stamped and stencilled with various paints. I like the look of burnt edges so I used a micro torch to singe the edge. (Use caution around flames.)

I used gel medium to adhere the fabric to the page. Place page under a heavy weight like an old book for a while to make sure the fabric adheres well. Add microbeads to some fabric edges.

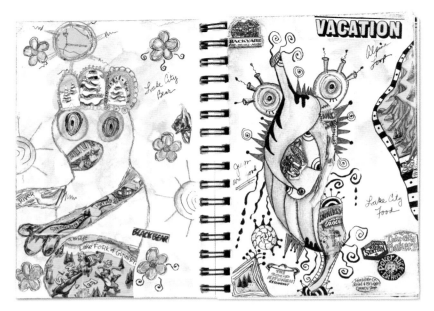

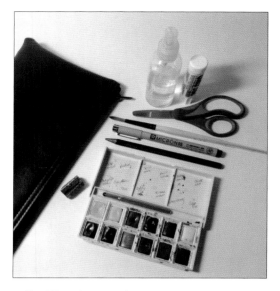

109. Spray Your Pages

I sprayed the pages with water, picked up different colors with a brush and applied them at random. After the water dried, I started drawing with markers and black Micron pens.

It is fun to let my pen draw and then look at the page to see where I need to add eyes and doodles. Note - My bear has 3 ears.

Minimal Materials

This is about making fun art with only a few supplies - a small spray bottle for water, a glue stick, scissors, a mini watercolor set, brush markers, a pencil, a pencil sharpener and maybe an eraser.

I drew images of my Colorado vacation - bears, food and the moose. For local images, I took a character map from the 'Welcome Center' cut out portions and glued it to the page.

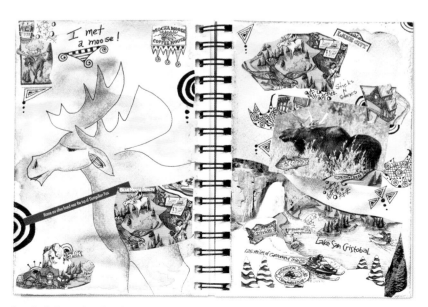

110. Memory Sketches

Combine hand drawings with simple sketches, a watercolor background, images from travel magazines and guide maps.

Decorate the pages with quick sketches. Your sketches don't need to be accurate... you just want to remember the essence and memories of your trip.

111. Napkins are Great

Napkins make great ephemera to add to a scrap page - use 2-ply or 1-ply. Most napkins can be peeled into two layers. The 1-ply is transparent enough to see through. The theme of my napkin was a chicken; it also had a cool border that I cut out to rim my page.

112. Save Everything

I love this fun tab from a family dinner at my favorite German restaurant, meant to be slipped on your drink when you take a potty break. This one went in my purse. Save even the smallest bits of memories. Of course I don't have to tell you that.. you're an artist.

Use Your Stash

My entire artistic being revolves around found objects, so I have a natural compulsion to use napkins, wine labels, postage stamps, postcards.... you name it.

Places I want to go are featured on this page. The underlying paper came from an old atlas. I doodled around my list with a paint marker and took my quote from Dr. Seuss.

Day of the Dead

I collect colorful Mexican folk art. I have always liked skeletons, and I'm really drawn to bright colors.

This page celebrates the 'Day of the Dead' tradition with images from my collection… jewelry pieces that I adore and collected stuff that I thought was fun.

As a kid, I loved Halloween. I used to dress up as zombies, Dracula, and scary stuff. Now I love skeletons.

113. Accordion Pages Show off my Collections

The accordion booklet is made from a page taken from a medical encyclopedia explaining the skeletal system. I crumpled it to give a distressed look, flattened it out and folded it. I burned the edges and glued one side to my page.

The black background paper is sprayed with Granite Mist to give it a dark sparkle. Using white paint, I made circles by dipping old jar lids into the paint. I wrote a favorite saying in with a Sharpie Poster Pen in blood red ink.

Open the booklet to reveal colors, your images and your words.

114. Magnets for Mix & Match

Magnets (from www.kjmagnetics.com) are available in all sizes and shapes. For the page background I used red cardstock and drew squiggles and swirls with a Silver paint marker. I attached my favorite cartoons by placing magnets on each side of the page.

115. Wake Up and Smell the Coffees
by Melissa Devenport

I love coffee with milk - cafe au lait. The Starbucks coffee sleeve has ridges that I used as a stamp with red paint. I border punched the coffee labels and used the rim of the coffee cup dipped in paint to make the circles.

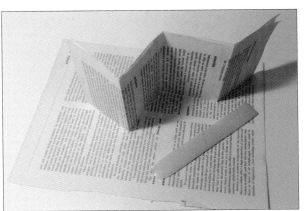

Tip - Go to library sales, estate sales, and Goodwill to find old Health Encyclopedias and other medical journals. They contain awesome images.

Accordion Booklet - Fold a page (approximately 9" x 12") from an old book in half lengthwise to 9" x 6". Next, fold it into 4 sections to make an accordion booklet (about 6" x 2¼" each).

Press the folds until crisp with a bone folder. Decorate the booklet, then glue one side to the page (see Day of the Dead page).

Duck Tape

Duck Tape is my favorite fix-all. It comes in a variety of colors and strengths, removable or permanent. Removable tape is perfect for temporary adhesions, like taping notes to a page. It's also good for auditioning images. If you don't like something, it's easily removable.

Purchase Duck Tape strong enough to reinforce the edge of a worn out binder or light enough to adhere vellum. I keep several kinds within reach on my art table.

116. Tic-Tac-Toe on a Black Page

This page began as a piece of black lined paper. Red Duck tape strengthens the punched edge. I did a chalk pastel rubbing over chipboard letters and applied spray fixative. Using Sharpie white and red Poster Pens.

117. Sheet Music

I laid a stencil over sheet music and spray painted. Then I adhered images with Duck tape.

Influence Poem

Splotch India ink onto page. Use an old twig to drag the ink into areas. Apply gold foil. Attach a poem.

118. Scraps & Tape

The back of a lot of scrap paper is just a blank page. I took colored Duck Tape and rolls of number tape to attach things I am saving just because I like them.

119. Lips

The lace and lips were a cover on an old spiral notebook. I backed it with paper and taped my favorite things to the page. The binder rings allow me to keep adding pages later.

No Rules

Scrapbookers have long been burdened by the "acid free" requirements. I'm here to release you from your bonds. Believe it or not, your Stash book can last a really long time, even if you hold it together with masking tape and glue.

Duck tape is your friend. If packing tape can survive the postal service, it won't harm your book. Besides, that newspaper clipping from 1929 that you just added to your page probably wasn't printed on acid free paper – and it didn't disintegrate.

Stash and Smash books are all about freedom. Here, you can do whatever inspires you. If you love fibers, string us along. If you love the texture of tissue and mulberry paper, go for it.

If it seems right to attach a note with Duck tape, rubber cement or gel medium, be fearless. This exploration is a no-holds-barred opportunity to explore paint, adhesives, papers, inks and every other medium you have ever wondered about.

What if I ruin it? You can't. There are no mistakes. If the paint runs thin, let it dry and add another coat. If you stamped something crooked, frame it. Make it look intentional. Don't judge, allow yourself to wonder at the possibilities for expression and freely explore.

This is your time. Make it a stress-free experience. If you begin to hesitate, turn the page, change the music, meditate for a moment, do a yoga posture or go for a walk. Preserving your confidence is the key to making progress.

Remember to breathe. Trust yourself.

Magazine Fabric for a Wrap Cover

by Ann Butler

Layers of torn magazine papers covered with sparkling paints combine beautifully to create a unique journal cover. This process is both fun and inexpensive, so you can enjoy making several.

MATERIALS:
Earth Safe Finishes Gel Medium
Earth Safe Finishes Shimmer Translucent paints
    (Copper, Gold Sparkle, Pearl)
Beacon Adhesives Fabri-Tac glue
Journal or hand-made book (about 8" x 9")
Magazine pages (good quality pages work best)
1/3 yard Muslin (depends on size of cover)
2 - 3 yards *Expo International* woven braid
Velcro Press and Seal Fasteners
Paintbrush, tooth pick, scissors, clothespins

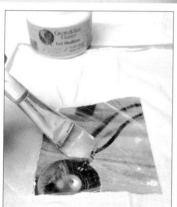   

Tear out colorful images from magazines. Use a paintbrush to apply gel medium to the back side of several pages. • Place wet pages onto muslin - overlap the edges. Apply gel medium to the top side of magazine pages. Continue until muslin is covered. • Apply 'Shimmer Translucent' paints over the magazine pages and let dry. • Apply Shimmer paints to the back side of muslin. Let dry. Add Shimmers until you are happy with the look - you can never add too much. Let dry.

INSTRUCTIONS:

1. Cut a 24" x 10" piece of muslin (this will cover an 8" x 9" journal or book).
   Note: Adjust the size of the muslin to fit another size of journal or book.
2. Make 'Magazine Fabric' on this piece of muslin. Let it dry overnight.
3. To make a 'Wrap Cover' fold one side of muslin about 3/4 of the way inside the front cover. Insert your journal in the pocket to be sure that it fits.
4. Wrap the long flap around the journal. Trim to fit. If desired cut the flap in a curve.
5. Use a toothpick to apply 'Fabri-Tac' glue. Adhere woven braid to the top side of muslin (magazine side). Use clothespins to hold trim in place while drying. Let dry.
6. Remove the journal. Use 'Fabri-Tac' glue to adhere the sides of the pocket together (wrong sides together). You can use clothespins to hold the sides together but this glue will dry fast. Let dry.
7. Adhere braid around the inside. Use clothespins to hold trim while drying. Let dry.
8. Slip a journal or book inside the pocket. Add Velcro spots to the cover as a closure.
9. For decoration, make a small loop from woven braid and glue it on top of the flap.

Ann Butler - Ann is a multi-talented designer. She specializes in air-dry clay, loves everything creative. She has a website at www.creativitystirsthesoul.com.
Ann can be contacted at am-designs@embarqmail.com

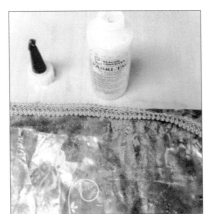

Use a toothpick to apply glue. Adhere woven braid to the top side of muslin (magazine side). Use clothespins to hold trim in place while drying. Let dry.

Stiffened Pages

I'm not destroying books and sheet music.

I'm restoring and reusing something so tattered it would have been thrown out in the trash.

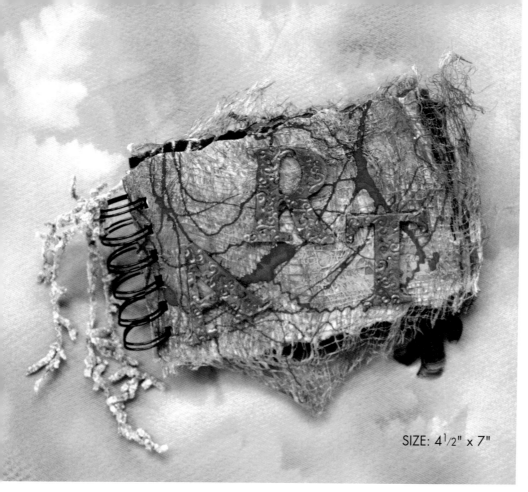

SIZE: 4 1/2" x 7"

Cover - Tear 140# watercolor paper to size. Use white glue to adhere old book pages to watercolor paper. Apply gesso in areas to add texture to the paper. Paint with watered-down Fluid acrylic paints. Use soft gel medium to adhere coffee dyed cheesecloth. Apply soft gel medium to cheesecloth hanging over the edges to stiffen it. Let dry. Apply Fluid acrylic paints randomly over the cheesecloth. Mix tar gel with Fluid acrylic paint and pour it onto the cover in swirl patterns.

Bind using a Zutter machine or have it bound at a print shop. Tie fibers to the binding rings.

Emboss Chipboard Letters with Textures - Spritz chipboard letters with water to wet it thoroughly. • Pound with leather stamp textures to make impressions. • Add color with acrylic paints. Antique with a darker color of acrylic paint. Rub this into the impressions, then wipe it off. Cover with gloss medium. Adhere to cover with regular gel medium.

120. Stiffened Sheet Music

I glued strips of fabric and scrap paper to stiffened sheet music. I coated the surface with matte medium to secure the embellishments. Now, instead of having a flimsy old page that is falling apart, I have something interesting and sturdy to use.

121. Brown Page

I hardened old gift wrap to make the brown page.

The gold accent is a tag with a fuzzy fiber ribbon attached.

   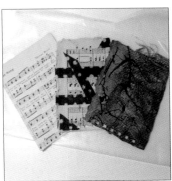

Stiffened Papers for Pages - The pages are made from stiffened napkins, gift wrap and old sheet music.
Fold a napkin, gift wrap, sheet music or other thin paper in half Cover the inside with white glue. • Sandwich the folded page between 2 sheets of wax paper. Pile heavy books on top. Allow to dry. • Create an assortment of stiffened papers.

Pockets for Pages

You've collected images, newspaper clippings, birthday cards, old gift wrap, grocery bags, postage stamps, report cards, copies of your birth certificate, and even the xray from the time you broke your arm. You know you will use it... sometime. How do you keep track of it all in the interim?

Pocket pages answer your storage needs. Big pockets keep sumptuous papers and exquisite vellums at hand while small pockets manage the memorabila of your life - napkins, advertising flyers, theatre tickets.

As you find related items in your pockets, the pocket page itself becomes a work of art, displaying your collection in an appealing fashion.

122. Tiered Pockets

Ripped and folded scrap papers become great tiers of storage as layered pockets for art class info.

123. Clever Title

Use paper sraps and fringed burlap to make this title. Hold it in place with gel medium.

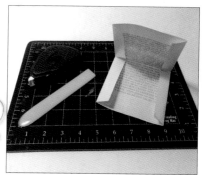

Option 1 - Fold a hem on each long side of a scrap paper and fold it in half. Glue the side flap together. • Option 2 - Trim the flaps off the top section. Fold it in half then glue the sides together • Punch a half circle in the center of one short edge (this makes removing paper easy). Attach pocket to the page with double-stick tape for a great storage pocket.